SUPER SUGAR

Written by
John Wood

BookLife PUBLISHING

©2021
BookLife Publishing Ltd.
King's Lynn
Norfolk PE30 4LS

All rights reserved.
Printed in Malta.

A catalogue record for this book is available from the British Library.

ISBN: 978-1-83927-488-6

Written by:
John Wood

Edited by:
William Anthony

Designed by:
Jasmine Pointer

All facts, statistics, web addresses and URLs in this book were verified as valid and accurate at time of writing. No responsibility for any changes to external websites or references can be accepted by either the author or publisher.

PHOTO CREDITS

All images are courtesy of Shutterstock.com, unless otherwise specified. With thanks to Getty Images, Thinkstock Photo and iStockphoto.

Scientist character throughout – Designbypex. Cover – Parilov, M. Unal Ozmen, Gita Kulinitch Studio, Tim UR. 4–5 – Ekaterina Kondratova. 6–7 – Bartolomiej Pietrzyk, 5 second Studio. 8–9 – Daniela Staerk, Martin Gardeazabal, dubassy, AlexeiLogvinovich, hanohiki. 10–11 – TY Lim. 12–13 – Ann in the uk, Rene Jansa. 14–15 – stockcreations, Evgeny Atamanenko. 16–17 – Dmitr1ch, Amelia Fox. 18–19 – Irina Suglobova, Tacar, Amelia Fox. 20–21 – EugenePut, mikeledray, Christina Grace, Sea Wave, anmbph, Amarita. 22–23 – Ildi Papp, Brent Hofacker, Michael C. Gray, Jiri Hera, ifong.

CONTENTS

Page 4   A Slice of Science
Page 6   Portions
Page 8   What Is Sugar?
Page 10   Let's Experiment!
Page 12   Nothing but the Tooth
Page 14   Sneaky Sugar
Page 16   Sugar in the Way
Page 18   Sugar Be Gone!
Page 20   Food Swaps
Page 23   The Most Important Thing
Page 24   Glossary and Index

Words that look like this can be found in the glossary on page 24.

A SLICE OF SCIENCE

Do you get told off for wanting to eat chocolate for breakfast? Do adults keep trying to feed you bananas? You might be wondering: why does it matter what I eat?

Hello! I'm a small scientist. I'm here to teach you about food. Food is very important!

You might have heard the words 'healthy diet'. A diet is the kinds of food you usually eat. To have a healthy diet, you need to make sure you eat the right amount of different food.

A healthy diet is often called a <u>balanced</u> diet because you eat lots of different types of food.

PORTIONS

But how do we <u>measure</u> the amount of food? A portion of food is the right amount you should eat in one sitting.

Sometimes portions are measured in grams. Use a scale like this to find out the right portion size.

A portion of food might be half a grapefruit.

Different foods have different portion sizes. You should have five portions of fruit and vegetables a day. A portion of fruit is roughly the amount you can fit in the palm of your hand.

WHAT IS SUGAR?

There are two types of sugar: <u>natural</u> sugars and free sugars.

Sugar is something found in food. It gives you <u>energy</u>. Having too much sugar can be bad for you, so it should only be a small part of your diet.

We should try to cut down on foods with free sugars in them. Here are a few examples.

Cookies

Sweets

Muffins

Doughnuts

LET'S EXPERIMENT!

> We will need this mood bar. It will tell us about someone's body. There are four things — how fast they are growing, <u>blood sugar</u> levels, how much they can concentrate and how healthy their teeth are.

GROWTH

BLOOD SUGAR

CONCENTRATION

TEETH

NOTHING BUT THE TOOTH

Here is the problem – too many fizzy drinks. Fizzy drinks often have a lot of sugar in them. Sugar damages our teeth, so we need to cut down on the amount of sugar we eat and drink.

Tooth decay can lead to teeth being taken out.

Let's have a look at the next child's mood bar. Their blood sugar levels are not normal. Let's find out what the problem is.

GROWTH

BLOOD SUGAR

CONCENTRATION

TEETH

SNEAKY SUGAR

This child is eating too much sugar – they could take some ice cream out of their diet. Eating too much sugar and not exercising can sometimes lead to <u>diseases</u> such as <u>diabetes</u> later in life.

A little bit of ice cream is OK as a treat.

Diabetes affects blood sugar levels, which can be dangerous.

SUGAR IN THE WAY

How about eating a bit less chocolate? A child needs <u>nutrients</u> to help their body grow. Sugary food such as chocolate doesn't have many nutrients and shouldn't be the main part of your diet.

SUGAR BE GONE!

We could try taking some cake out of her diet. Cakes are very sugary, and sugar doesn't give you energy for a very long time. This means you may get tired quickly and find it harder to concentrate.

Wholegrain cereal is much better at giving you energy for a longer time.

FOOD SWAPS

We can swap sugary foods for healthier snacks. Instead of eating chocolate or biscuits, why not try some of these foods?

Cucumber sticks

Sugar free jelly

Here are a few more foods with free sugar in. Try not to eat too much of this kind of food.

Jelly

Custard

Pudding

Sugary cereals

THE MOST IMPORTANT THING

Eating sugary foods can be a treat, but don't forget that you must eat lots of different types of food. This is what makes a diet healthy and balanced.

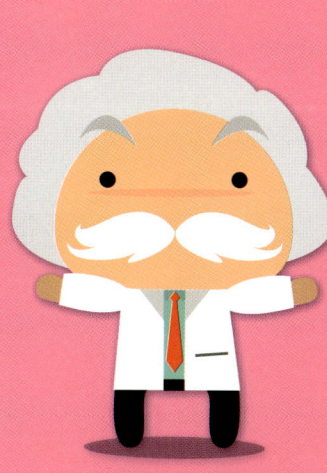

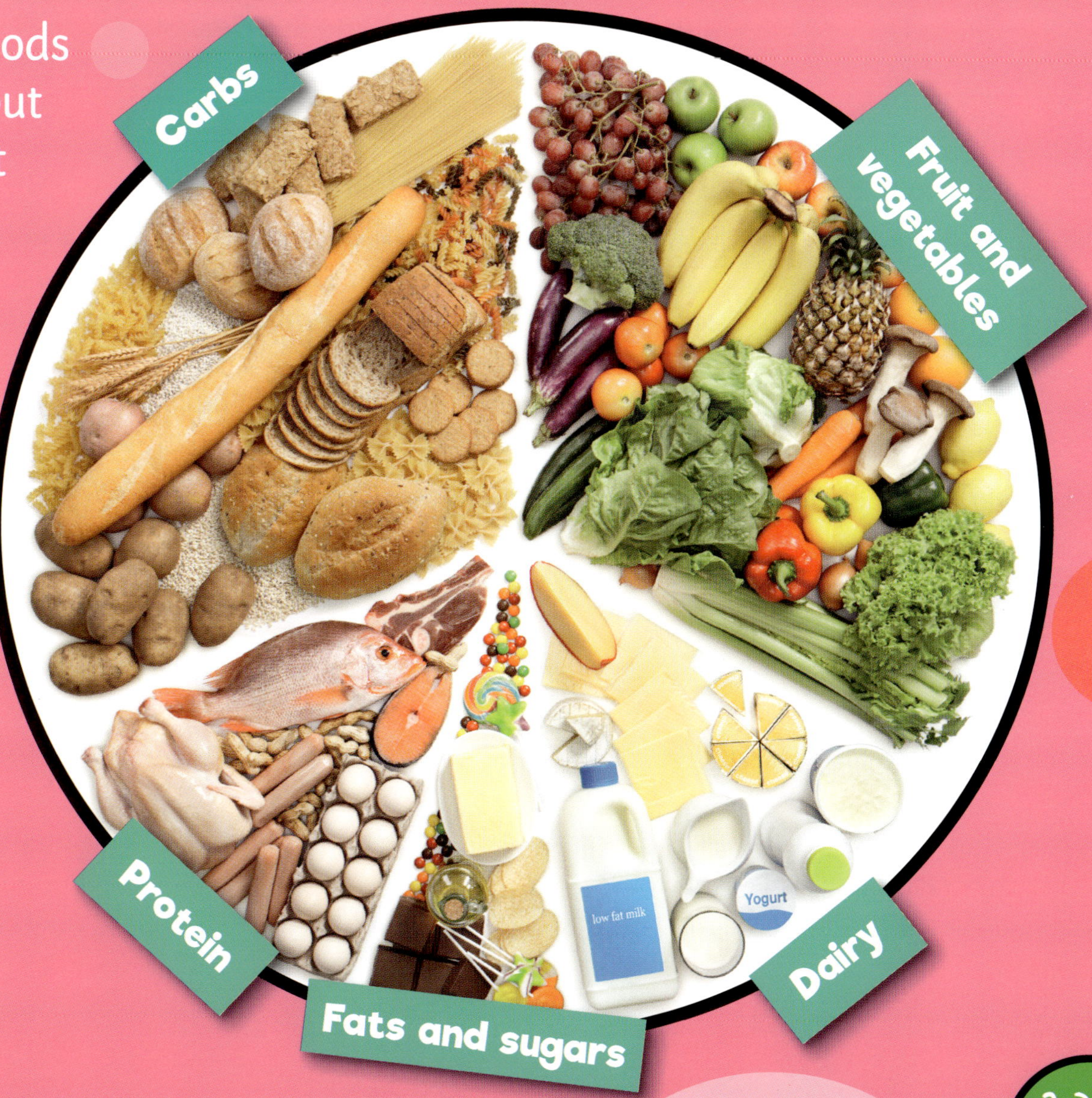
Carbs
Fruit and vegetables
Protein
Fats and sugars
Dairy
low fat milk
Yogurt

GLOSSARY

balanced	made up of the right or equal amounts
blood sugar	a type of sugar that is transported around the body in your blood
damages	breaks or causes harm
diabetes	a disease in which the body has trouble controlling blood sugar levels, which can lead to damage to organs
diseases	illnesses that cause harm to the health of a person
energy	the ability to do something
measure	find out the exact amount of something using units or systems, such as grams for weight or metres for distance
natural	found in nature and not made by people
nutrients	things that plants and animals need to grow and stay healthy
tooth decay	when the outer layer of a tooth is destroyed or broken by germs
wholegrain	contains the whole of the grain seed and all of the nutrients

INDEX

blood sugar 10, 13–14
cake 18
chocolate 4, 16, 20
concentration 10, 17–18
dairy 14, 21, 23
diet 5, 8, 14, 16, 18, 23
diseases 14
eggs 21
fizzy drinks 12
fruit 4, 7, 21, 23
growing 10, 15–16
ice cream 14
portions 6–7
sweets 9
tiredness 18
vegetables 7, 20–21, 23